Where We Live

India

Donna Bailey and Malcolm Rodgers

STECK-VAUGHN
LIBRARY
A Division of Steck-Vaughn Company

Hello! My name is Sita.

I live on a farm in Rajasthan.

Rajasthan is in northwest India.

2

Rajasthan is a very dry part of India.
Some of it is a desert.
The people who live in the desert cannot
grow any crops because the land is too dry.
They keep camels and goats instead.

We live where it is not so dry.
But we do have to water our crops.
We bring water up from our well
with this special wheel.
Then we can water the fields and
keep the crops growing.

4

Our farm is just outside the city of Jaipur.
Jaipur is the capital of Rajasthan.
My grandparents, uncles, and aunts
all live on the farm with us.
Everyone helps with the farm work.

Dad grows wheat on the farm.
We make our own flour from the wheat.
Mom makes bread and pancakes called
chapatis with the flour.

We grow vegetables near the house.
My sister helps care for the
vegetable garden.

We also have cows on the farm.

My brother helps Dad with the cows.

He milks them every morning and afternoon.

My aunt makes butter and cheese
from the milk.

We use oxen to pull the cart when
Dad wants to take our wheat, vegetables,
and butter to sell in Jaipur.
We also use them to plow the fields.

When Dad goes to Jaipur, he gets up
very early.
He loads up the cart and
hitches up the oxen.
Sometimes he has a calf to sell,
as well as wheat and other things.

I like going with Dad to Jaipur.
I ride on the cart beside him.
The oxen walk very slowly, so
Dad has to crack his whip.
The sudden noise makes them go faster.

Sometimes there is a cattle market
near Jaipur.
The farmers sell their calves and
cattle in the market.

Jaipur is a large city with many
carts, cars, and bicycles in the streets.
There are many small stores and stalls, too.

Some stores sell food and vegetables.
Others sell clothes, flowers, and
things people have made.

14

Artisans in Jaipur make beautiful
wood carvings and brass trays.
They decorate the trays with
many patterns.

My uncle makes clothes and saris
in his shop.
Saris are traditional dress for women in India.
Jaipur women like to wear saris
at festivals and weddings.

16

The women wear their most colorful clothes
and prettiest jewels when
they go to weddings.
There is always music and dancing.
The women like dancing at weddings.
They also dance at all the Hindu festivals.

17

One of the most important Hindu festivals
is the festival of Diwali.
It takes place in late October or
early November, when the moonless nights
are very dark.

Diwali is a time when everyone in
the family tries to get together.
First, people get their houses ready
for the festival.
In the weeks before Diwali, people
are busy cleaning and decorating their homes.

In some houses the women make
beautiful patterns on their floors
with a colored rice-flour paste.
There are many different patterns.

People make these patterns to ask for
the blessing of the goddess Lakshmi.
They believe Lakshmi visits the houses at Diwali
and brings good luck for the coming year.

Some families set up a small shrine
to Lakshmi in their homes.
They put decorations, flowers, and candles
around a statue of Lakshmi.

People buy garlands of fresh flowers
to decorate their statues of Lakshmi.
They also decorate the entrances to
their stores and homes.

Diwali lasts from three to five days.
During this time, hundreds of lamps are lit
each evening in all the towns
and villages throughout India.

24

Some people use colored electric lights
to decorate their houses.
Others make Diwali lamps from
little clay pots.

They fill the lamps with oil
and light the floating wicks.
People put their Diwali lights on
every ledge and shelf, both inside and
outside their homes.

Before Diwali, people buy new clothes.
The women wear their best saris and
put flowers and perfume in their hair.
They buy lots of colored bracelets
to match their new clothes.

During Diwali every town and village has a fair.
Crowds of people come from all around.
There are sideshows and Ferris wheels to ride on.

There are stalls where people can buy
hot, spicy food or sweet, sticky snacks.
The sweets are made from
boiled milk and sugar.
They are flavored with nuts,
fruits, and raisins.

At some stalls women can have
beautiful patterns painted on their hands.
The patterns are painted with a brown dye
called henna.

Acrobats, snake charmers, and jugglers
entertain the people at the fair.
There is also music and dancing.
In the evening there are fireworks displays.

On the last day of Diwali, families
gather for a special feast.
They all exchange gifts
of candy wrapped in silver paper.

Index

Reading Consultant: Diana Bentley
Editorial Consultant: Donna Bailey
Supervising Editor: Kathleen Fitzgibbon

Illustrated by Gill Tomblin
Picture research by Suzanne Williams
Designed by Richard Garratt Design

Photographs
Cover: Robert Harding Picture Library
Robert Harding Picture Library: 4, 6, 16, 29
The Hutchison Library: 7, 14, 22, 26, 27, 28
Ann & Bury Peerless: 1, 2, 3, 5, 8, 9, 15, 20, 21, 30, 32
Rex Features: 13, 17
Library of Congress Cataloging-in-Publication Data: Bailey, Donna. [India] India / Donna Bailey and
Malcolm Rodgers; [illustrated by Gill Tomblin]. p. cm. —(Where we live) Previously published as:
We live in India. SUMMARY: Depicts the life of a farm girl of dry northwest India, and portrays life in the
city of Jaipur, especially during the festival of Diwali. ISBN 0-8114-2548-7 1. India—Social life and
customs—Juvenile literature. [1. India—Social life and customs.] I. Rodgers, Malcolm. II. Tomblin, Gill, ill.
III. Title. IV. Series. DS421.B19   1990   954—dc20   89-26122   CIP   AC